Table of Contents

INTRODUCTION

Permaculture is an innovative framework for creating sustainable ways of living. It is a practical method of developing ecologically harmonious, efficient and productive systems that can be used by anyone, anywhere.

By thinking carefully about the way we use our resources - food, energy, shelter and other material and non-material needs - it is possible to get much more out of life by using less. We can be more productive for less effort, reaping benefits for our environment and ourselves, for now and for generations to come.

This is the essence of permaculture - the design of an ecologically sound way of living - in our households, gardens, communities and businesses. It is created by cooperating with nature and caring for the earth and its people.

Permaculture encourages us to be resourceful and self-reliant. It is not a dogma or a religion but an ecological design system which helps us find solutions to the many problems facing us - both locally and globally.

CHAPTER ONE

Permaculture Design

Nature provides the best examples we have of complex systems that are not just abundant, but resilient and self-balancing too. Indeed we are completely surrounded by examples of excellent practice – including our own bodies. Yet it's clear from the imbalances that we are now creating in natural systems, that our recent human actions haven't been quite so well designed. We know we can do better, and the feedback that we are receiving is part of our education.

The fast pace of modern life means that while we may look, we don't always see. Our attention span gets shorter as we reach information overload, and yet the things we often notice the least are the very things keeping us alive, day in, day out. To turn things around, we have to learn to see again, which is why permaculture urges us to become better observers. Starhawk shares nine different ways for us to do this in her book, The Earth Path and nature awareness training also has many such gifts to share. Observation skills were vital for our ancestors just to stay alive and despite our seemingly cosy modern lives, that may not be so far from the truth for us to- day either. The dangers may be less apparent to us, but unheeded they could be just as deadly.

Thankfully, many of us are already being good lookouts for humanity, pointing out the potential dangers of climate change and peak oil† to others. As astute observers of what has been going wrong, we're also part of the way to creating solutions. We just need to learn from our mistakes and see where we could make better choices in the future. Good observation is an important skill for us to have in gathering information that enables us to create those better designs, and we'll need it to monitor the effectiveness of our subsequent creations too.

One of the first things we notice when we observe natural ecosystems is that certain patterns keep appearing, in many situations and at varying scales. These patterns occur in both time and space, and while the former determine our routines, the latter are often only considered for their beauty. However, nature's most common patterns have evolved over many millennia† as being the most effective for survival. While conditions on the surface of the Earth have changed considerably over time, life has always managed to adapt in order to survive and thrive here. So our challenge as designers is to identify what each of these patterns excels at doing and to apply them where appropriate in our designs.

Patterns in space

The study of patterns and their successful application in design is a fascinating and detailed subject much beyond the scope of this guide. That said, there are some key principles that, once understood, can help us to use them effectively in our designs. Firstly, patterns occur at the edge between two different media or systems. So the branching fractal form of a broccoli head is simply the edge between the plant and the atmosphere, the waves on the ocean the place at which the air mixes with the water. Resources are exchanged across these edges; needs are met and waste products eliminated, so by increasing surface area, nature increases the efficiency of this interaction and ultimately the size and health of the organism. Hence we find that many of the most common patterns we see around us in nature (branching, waves, spirals, webs and so on), all have extensive 'edge'. Of course the ultimate edge on this beautiful planet is the one between the earth and the atmosphere where almost everything lives, and that's because this is where all the key requirements for life occur together.

Observation skills

Think about what soil actually is – minerals from the earth, mixing with gases from the atmosphere, and water from both regions. This is why healthy soil has to have a good structure, in other words lots of edge, in order to support life! Life in turn speeds up the interaction between the earth and the atmosphere; plants and trees in particular, considerably increasing the surface area of exchange between these two media through the branching of their top growth and root systems. Thus, these translators keep energy and resources such as sunlight, minerals, water and gases on the move across this familiar edge; harvesting sufficient to grow and make themselves ever more effective at performing this service, while also building soil as a by-product, which in turn supports more life.

Of course there are times too when minimising edge (to reduce exchange) is advantageous. When a woodlouse curls into a ball for protection, or a cat curls up to retain body heat, we see this occurring. As well as having the least edge, spheres are also the most stable form, and yet nature is always looking for ways to increase that edge while maintaining a dynamic stability. A cell will stretch to increase its surface area and upon reaching a point of instability will divide into two stable forms again, but now with a greater combined surface area. This process occurs over and over again, in a pulsing form. Our own bodies are only prevented from returning to a stable spherical blob by our investment in a skeleton to keep us elongated. Many other life forms develop similar structures to increase their surface area.

Even the surface of the Earth, though close to spherical in form, is constantly being disturbed by tectonic activity pushing up mountain ranges and by wind driving up waves on the oceans. Those great mountain ranges are gradually ground down by the forces of nature, into smaller and smaller pieces, with each fracture increasing the edge upon which life can take hold. So contrary to our fear of things falling apart, this breaking down process actually provides more opportunities for life.

We've been taught to fear entropy, but without this process there'd be no raw materials for life to create itself anew with. The 'Lobular' pattern that results from weathering is what makes a well-structured soil fertile and such an effective cleaner of water overloaded with faeces; a pattern we mimic in using gravel beds to do this job in sewage treatment works, gravel providing a substantial surface area on which bacteria that break down sewage can live. We find the same pattern again at work in our own colons, where bacteria pre-digest our food for us through their huge collective surface area. Don't forget that decomposers perform the vital recycling role within ecosystems.

We see many patterns of beneficial interaction around us in nature. Our own bodies are of course prime examples of the value of successful co-operative relationships between cells. In addition to an abundance of multi-cellular organisms, nature abounds with symbioses – close and often long-term interactions between different biological species – and we can identify patterns in the ways that they interact with each other. Even apparently parasitic relationships reveal their mutualisms upon closer inspection. Ivy is often blamed for killing trees and cut down to stop this occurring. But how can such a relatively small plant ever overwhelm a large healthy tree? Ivy provides important wildlife habitat and cutting it causes more harm than good. Careful study reveals that it only overwhelms trees that are already dying, the tree no longer out-competing the ivy for nutrients. From this point it provides an important ecosystem service by increasing the wind load on the tree and bringing it more quickly back to the earth where it can be turned back into soil to feed new life – particularly important in cool temperate climes where this process is already a relatively slow one.

Entropy is often viewed as an unstoppable destructive force to be feared and fought at all costs. We fear our food rotting and our cars and our houses falling apart, hence our invention of preservatives and non-biodegradable plastics. However, these things lock up vital biological nutrients, needed to make new life.

Then again, are these bacteria separate or actually part of us? Some scientists now believe that 90% of the cells in our bodies are microbes, mainly bacteria.

So by studying what makes nature successful we can derive principles of ecology that guide us in mimicking nature's strategies. Life is always looking to increase any beneficial interactions, and energy and resources are kept on the move.† This makes for an abundant and stable, but complex system.

Patterns in time

These are more familiar, as our lives inevitably revolve around our responses to them. Primary (driving) patterns, such as the seasons and day/night cycles, elicit secondary (responding) patterns in life by way of adaptation. In the temperate and polar regions, plants adapt to seasonal changes by growing when there is sufficient heat, light and moisture, and becoming dormant when there is a lack. This in turn drives the behaviour of the species that feed on those plants, and who have evolved three main strategies to survive through the winter months.

Each strategy takes advantage of the autumn abundance of available food. Some put on weight to stick it out foraging through the winter, some hibernate and some migrate. Perhaps our ancestors once migrated too, but for those of us now living in those regions, our permanent dwelling places offer us a new form of hibernation. Alas, we now use an- cient sunlight (fossil fuels) to heat them, which may be a more energy-expensive choice than migration. Not that we have that choice anymore as our species now covers the whole Earth – there's nowhere else for us to go...

By studying temporal patterns we can now more accurately predict the arrival of spring, the best times to plant seeds for a good harvest and how much time we have to build our home before the inclement weather arrives. Sadly, many of our current human systems such as our nine to five work patterns, still take no account of seasonal and daily fluctuations in our energy levels. A redesign is in order! Energy in all its forms needs to keep moving in order to avoid stagnation e.g. moving water carries more dissolved oxygen and thus supports more life.

An Introduction to systems

A basic understanding of the way systems behave is one key to good design. Actually there's a whole inter-disciplinary theory called Systems Theory dedicated to this, which studies the way complex systems behave in nature, society and science. It's an important piece of the permaculture puzzle and Howard T. Odum, an early proponent of Systems Ecology, was a clear influence on David Holmgren's early thinking.

So when we put specific things (elements) together (into systems), how do they behave (function)? Well to consider this, let's choose an example very close to home; our own digestive system (systems are often named after their primary function).

While we've all experienced how it feels when it struggles with our food choices, some of us are a little more familiar than others about the finer details of its functioning. So which elements would you say make up our digestive system? Well, it depends upon whom you ask. Have a look in some medical text books or do an image search on the Internet and you'll get a variety of answers. Some diagrams show only abdominal organs, while others include the mouth, salivary glands etc. too. This discrepancy comes from the fact that while the human body ‡ as a whole has a clearly defined edge, the sub-systems (of which this is one) do not. I chose this diagram (left) as it includes the tongue, teeth and oft-forgotten nose. Our sense of smell is actually an important component of taste. This sense in turn ensures that the materials we place into our mouth are suitable for digestion, thus acting as an important filter for not just the digestive system, but the body as a whole.

So it's actually quite difficult to define exactly what constitutes the digestive system, as we can see the edge between it and the other sub-systems of the body is rather subjective. We could make the same observation about the respiratory system, the circulatory system, the reproductive system and so on. This is because elements (or sub-systems†) within systems are often multi-functional, each performing some important, sometimes vital, functions across sub-systems and ultimately supporting the whole, while at the same time being supported by the whole.

Remove the digestive system from the body and it would quickly perish, as would the rest of the body left behind. So while it can be useful sometimes to conceptually sub-divide systems to make their interactions easier to consider, we mustn't lose sight of the fact that no part of a system ever exists totally in isolation. Even the smallest elements within systems could be performing functions vital to the health and stability of the overall system and also be totally dependent upon it. Imagine life without your eyes, your thumbs or even the semicircular canals in your ears that allow you to keep your balance.

So, as permaculture designers we always aim to make small changes, first observing the effects that making these has on the system, and ensuring that they're beneficial, before going further. Compare this to modern corporate-driven practices that expose us all to rapid changes in our environment such as significantly raised levels of electromagnetic radiation from computers and mobile phones etc. We've not had enough time to observe the possible side-effects of fields that simply don't exist in nature. This occurs because someone wants to make a 'quick buck' before their competitors get in on the market.

Because of the complexity of systems, we often find it difficult to see the whole picture of what is going on. So another key thing we should know is that systems can sometimes behave very unpredictably (look at how unreliable weather forecasts can be, even with all the computing power now available to meteorologists).

While the elements that make up a system may all act in one direction, the combination of them all may act in a completely different way. It's also important to notice whereabouts we find elements within systems. All non-human life makes everything using locally sourced resources and expertise – and that doesn't mean food from within a 50 mile radius (try walking or even cycling that on a regular basis). No, we find species thriving only where nature provides for their needs and where their waste products can be reused. If we move species elsewhere, we risk creating an imbalance in the local ecology.

In the same way, if we move or remove any element from a system, we might throw it out of balance or stop it functioning completely. Imagine if your teeth were moved to between your stomach and intestines. We might then find our digestion performed a little less well. Things need to be in the right location. Remove our teeth completely and, well some of us already know how that is. At least we can still manage to some degree without teeth, but lose our liver function and we're in real trouble...

Systems also always have functions.† Observing a system over time allows us to determine what those functions are (and in hu- man-designed systems, such as financial institutions and corporations, it's not always what they purport to be!).

The Yellowstone Wolves

For nearly 70 years wolves that inhabited this great nature re- serve were missing – hunted and killed by humans. Over that period, elk increased in number and became sickly beasts. Young trees were failing to replace the old because of the extra grazing and the forests were dying. In 1985, 31 wolves were released back into the park and in the 25 years since elk numbers have returned to former levels. The herds are fitter because they move much more and the forests are growing back. Beavers have re- turned too – relying on a good growth of willow at the water's edge. In turn the dams they make have slowed river flow, reducing the loss of soil through run off and lowering the risk of down- stream flooding. All of this occurred because of the wolves.

For most systems, one of the key functions is 'to ensure its own perpetuation'. Hence in permaculture we aim to obtain a yield and also a surplus for reinvestment. The overall functions of systems are determined not just by the functions of the elements or sub-systems that they are composed of, but also the interconnections (relationships) between them. All elements in a system can be replaced (e.g. cells in the human body, people in a university), but if the interconnections remain the same, the system will continue to function in the same way.

These interconnections are what makes any system strong (like a web), but also more complex. This makes sense of our desire to simplify things as much as possible, so we have less to think about (monoculture farming is a perfect example of this). How- ever, simpler systems are far less resilient and more vulnerable to outside changes, like a reduction in the availability of one or more important inputs, such as oil. In contrast, a web or interconnect- ed system can have over half its threads break and still be able to successfully harvest resources.

Feedback

Another key principle of systems is that these interconnections often create loops that feedback on themselves, which either oppose or support any change. The first kind of feedback keeps a system in balance and these of course abound in Nature. They keep everything vital to life, such as oxygen levels, temperature, etc. consistently at the right levels. They work by creating an opposing reaction when something changes, bringing it back to a point of balance. One example of this is how we continually adjust our posture, in order to stay upright as we walk or ride a bike, especially on a windy day. In fact when we first learn to do these things, we are simply training our body's feedback mechanisms to keep us upright.

The second kind of feedback is a reinforcing process, where any movement away from a point of balance stimulates a further move- ment away. Crossing your hands over on the handlebars of a bike demonstrates this very effectively, though speaking from personal experience.

An epidemic is another such scenario; the more infectious people there are, the quicker a disease spreads. After birth, a feedback mechanism is set in motion whereby we grow to the size determined by our environment to be ideal, and then at puberty the release of hormones creates feedback that keeps us at this opti- mum size. Balancing loops keep systems at a steady state and reinforcing ones move them from one steady state to another.

While at first, reinforcing feedback processes may not seem as common as balancing ones, we can actually find plenty of examples of them around us, many as a result of our human actions. Much of the work we have to do to repair eco-systems involves identifying and reversing destructive, reinforcing feedback loops that our relatively recent human activities have set into motion.

Spirals of erosion and degradation

Anything that we value, but that is being progressively lost; from soil to silence, from biodiversity to darkness, from trees to a sense of purpose, can be studied to help us identify the root causes of these problems.

Of course, the latter approach involves extra time and effort, which is 'more than necessary' to councils and governments who only have a few years to convince us they are worth voting for again. So each successive regime patches up the mess the last lot left behind, as cheaply as possible and with no thought for the longer-term future. Not a recipe for success.

So it's up to us as individuals to see the folly in this thinking and come up with something better. Which brings us back to evaluating why any given thing doesn't work and where we can make different choices. Take for example, using a rotavator to clear 'weeds' from an allotment plot. In the short term it does what is intended, but chops perennial 'weed' roots, propagating them in the process and also brings dormant weed seeds to the surface. This ultimately means more 'weeds', which leads to more rotavating. Until that is, the oil runs out...

Now this is a very simple reinforcing loop (which spirals more and more out of control) – 'weeds' stimulate rotavating, which in turn leads to more 'weeds', then more rotavating and so on. An obvious point of intervention here would be to choose a different method of control. However, many loops are a little more complex than this and require a bit more consideration.

Start thinking about some of these loops for yourself. Pick something familiar that you see being eroded; perhaps local community, food growing knowledge, letter writing etc. and see if you can draw the spiral that has caused the problem. What interventions could you make to turn the problem around? Identifying the root causes of what we might also refer to as resource or energy leaks, provides us with one or more points at which we can begin to address them. We'll return to this later when we're figuring out what the functions of our design are going to be.

Next time you find yourself with a group of friends (ideally at least ten of you), try this interesting exercise. You might start by standing in a circle, facing inwards. Explain that each of you needs to think of two other people in the group (but not to reveal who they are). Then explain that when the game starts they need to simply make an equilateral (equal sided) triangle with those two other people. Choose two people from the circle to demonstrate and move to form such a triangle with them both. Also point out that you could walk between them and make a triangle from the other side of them too. Of course, each of the people who are in your triangle will soon be moving to make triangles of their own!

The great value in having principles and directives is that we can use them to easily apply successful natural patterns to the many things we do. The simplest way to do this is to use the principles of ecology in designing gardens and farms and I'd recommend this as being a good place to start. However, we can be more creative and apply many of these same principles beyond land-based design too, something I'll give examples of in part three.

Permaculture also addresses how we think, the mess we see around us being simply a reflection of the mess in our heads. Then again, our modern lifestyle has so disconnected us from nature that perhaps we shouldn't be so surprised. So having some principles of attitude can assist our approach and help us to see the hidden gifts in every situation. I'll be introducing some of these principles at the most relevant places in the text.

Effective Design

So what exactly is design and how can permaculture help us to do it well?

Design is the conscious assembly of concepts, materials, techniques and strategies for a particular purpose. Seeing all the exciting possibilities that permaculture offers us, it's easy to forget this and just end up throwing together a collection of 'green' technologies and techniques, only to be disappointed by the result. There's now no shortage of these 'green options' for us to choose from and we've been given the impression that as long as we behave in certain ways and buy the right products, we're doing the best we can.

But permaculture and design is about more than just choosing the right things, it's also about how we connect them together. Nature abounds with examples of beneficial relationships, showing us the value of this strategy for long-term sustainability. So as permaculture designers, our role is to place components in the best places relative to each other, to create self-sustaining systems that also meet our needs. However, such relationships are often site-related, so we need to be able to consciously design; to become a 'permaculture chef', rather than simply learning to follow a recipe.

Permaculture tells us that when we design to meet our needs, we should do so in a way that supports the ecosystem as a whole, without which we are as doomed as that digestive system placed in isolation. Of course, permaculture is not a specific recipe, nor an end point. Rather it is an ongoing process of harmonious adap- tation to nature's changing conditions. The design process can help us each to find and stay on our own path.

Techniques are simply how we do things. Choosing the right techniques depends upon a good knowledge of the limits of the eco-system in which we are working.

Strategies then add time, defining when we do things. This requires a knowledge of seasonal variations.

Design then adds where to the equation, placing things in the best location and in an optimum relationship to each other.

Everything gardens – While we may currently be making a bit of a mess of things, it's perfectly natural for us to be shaping our environment to meet our needs. Biomimicry advocate Janine Benyus points out that even when our choices appear anything but natural, as a product of nature we can't ever do anything else. Instead she asks whether our choices are well- adapted ones. Permaculture gives us the tools to create systems that support not only ourselves, but future generations too and Life as a whole.

Identifying roles within the process

Now let's consider the roles each person will take within the design process. Sometimes, as both designer and client, you might find yourself the only person designing and implementing a particular project. In which case, you can skip ahead a few pages to the section on Design Frameworks.

Whenever you do find yourself working for or with others though, in order to avoid confusion and conflict, it helps to define everyone's roles at the beginning of the process. In such a situation, you might be:

* Working as a sole designer or part of a team.

* Working for a single client or multiple clients.

* Also responsible for delivering the implementation of your design, either as project manager or as the workforce.

We'll look at some tools to help with the first situation in a moment, the second we'll address in the Client Interview chapter and the third under Implementation, towards the end of part two.

Whenever designing for clients, it's advisable that you, or the agreed leader of your team, should clarify these details with them before you start, in writing in a design proposal.

Such a document should:

* Clarify the permaculture ethics and principles underlying the design process, in the context of the design.

* Include an overview of the design process itself.

* Define the agreed roles of the client(s).

* Outline your fees (daily rate / estimated timescale).

* Perhaps provide short biographies of the designers.

* Identify the point at which your involvement ends.

The Design Process

All design frameworks begin with observing and recording and we should give good attention to this stage as it informs all the decisions we'll make later. Whereas most of us currently spend just 20% of our time planning and implementing something and then 80% maintaining it, in permaculture we set out to change those numbers around. Ironically the gift of oil has made us far more wasteful of energy, something our ancestors would never have done for long. We've used fossil fuels to replace skill with brute force in so many areas, particularly in food production. Thankfully, we haven't com- pletely lost those skills yet and there are a few inspirational farmers who have a lot to teach us about using our resources wisely. They all understand that a well-designed system should, more or less, look after itself, though intensive food production inevitably involves a certain amount of interaction on our part, 'Harvesting as maintenance' being the Holy Grail of design.

While this process can be applied to designing more than just landscapes (more about that in part three) we'll start off by doing this, as it's the easiest way to get a sense of the flow. In the land-based example we'll be following, the observation is made in two parts; first of the land and then of the client(s).

Look at a site before interviewing any client(s) in detail. This gives you an unclouded view of what you see there. The survey also often raises questions that may need further clarification, such as issues around the history of use of the site. So doing it this way around makes most sense to me. However, this isn't a hard and fast rule, and you'll have to ask the client(s) in advance about site boundaries anyway (so you know exactly where you're surveying!). When you do so, ask them if they already have a good map of the site that you can adapt for your own use. If they do have one it will save you mapping time later.

If you're designing for yourself, you'll already have a fairly clear idea of what you want, and if the site is familiar to you, a good sense of what is there. Then this process becomes one of clarification and expansion. It's your design process, so find the way that works best for you; be careful that you don't let your design ideas cloud your observations though! Enlisting a friend less familiar with the space, to add their own observations, can often illicit a new way of seeing familiar spaces. Such outside perspectives can help you sweep away blocks that had previously been limiting your ability to see the most obvious issues.

The main thing to remember here is that a little extra time spent observing now is going to save you a whole lot of effort later. Bill Mollison suggests observing our design site for at least one full cycle. For a land-based project, that means of course a whole year. However, if you don't have all that information to hand, there may be others who can help you fill in the gaps. Neighbours and previous owners may also know where the sunniest and shadiest areas are and where and when it floods or frosts etc. They might well have photographs that allow you to look back in time. Include these people as part of your client interview process if you can.

The Site Survey

Maps

To design well, you always have to get onto the site, that said it helps to have a framework in which to record observations and maps can provide that for us. Hopefully your client can provide you with a map that you can use for this purpose, but if not there are still plenty of places from which you can obtain a useful one, including online services.† However, even if you're fortunate enough to be holding such a map in your hand, it's unlikely that it will be the perfect one for you just yet.

Maps are made for different reasons, so any you have will include some irrelevant things and lack other important data. What you need to know will vary of course depending upon where and what you are de- signing. For instance, having detailed contour information can save a lot of time survey- ing a large property, whereas it's unlikely you'll need to know this if you are designing a small urban garden.

Even having the basic outline of a site can be a helpful starting point, saving you a significant amount of surveying time in determining the boundaries, size and shape of the plot. It's important though to remember that maps are just a snapshot in time and may no longer be accurate. Only by visiting the site itself will you be able to determine this. Perhaps the only old maps that can be relied upon are those mapping geology and soils.

So first identify what it is that you need to know and then investigate which maps are available that already contain this information. Remember, the right map can pay for itself many times over by saving you time spent gathering particular data. This is especially important if you're working to a budget. It's worth mentioning here that aerial photographs can also be useful, though care should be taken with those provided by free online mapping sites as they can be distorted at the point where individual photos are stitched together to create a seam- less landscape. Sometimes the seam is obvious, such as when images were taken at different times of year (one issue with projecting an unnatural cloud-free landscape I suppose). You also should check such maps are up to date; at the time of writing, the Google MapsTM aerial photo of our home still shows it before it was extended by the last owner – over five years ago!

DIY mapping

There may be times when you won't have access to an exist- ing map at a useful scale and you'll have to create your own. This is a useful skill to have anyway, so no mapmaking task is ever a waste of time. Although 100% accuracy is always worth aiming for, getting close to that can often be disproportionally time consuming. In practice 90-95% is good enough for most situations, with perhaps contouring for water management being one key exception – however nicely you ask it, water never flows uphill unaided!

Urban garden designs usually include a considerable amount of detail, planting schemes etc. and so need to be surveyed accurately enough to ensure that any proposed garden beds and paths will all fit into the given space. Broader scale (e.g. farm) designs are often more pattern based, addressing how separate systems can be connected together in the most effective way. Slight inaccuracies in DIY mapping may only lead to the need to plant a few more trees in a hedge line, and it's worth remembering that the final canopy sizes of trees given in books will always be approximate and site dependent. That said, paying for an accurately contoured map can allow you to for instance, design and precisely lay out a Keyline® system† on the ground using an affordable GPS unit.

Making base and field maps

As well as needing a map to communicate our design ideas, we also need one onto which we can record the information we'll be gathering. We call this our base map. It should be simple, mapping site boundaries and 'fixed' elements like buildings, roads, significant bodies of water and large trees. In addition it should include a scale for the map, the direction of north, the place and the date.

Create a base map from an existing map

If you've already found a good map, this should be a relatively simple process, but you'll still have to pick out the information you need and probably enlarge it too. Assuming the map is still accurate (and they won't always be), you should first scale it up to a useful size. You're going to need both a base map that you can present your ideas on later and a smaller field map that you can record information onto whilst on site. These will almost certainly need to be at different scales. Site work will usually involve using a clipboard, whereas design presentations, especially to a group of people, are better done at a larger scale.

Extend the boundaries

A good method for expanding or simply copying a map is to use a large window as a makeshift light box. Obviously this only works during the day! Tape your existing (smaller) map onto the inside of the window and then your larger sheet of paper fairly centrally over the top, so you can see through the big sheet to the small map underneath. Place a dot on your big paper somewhere over the middle of the smaller map beneath; this will act as the reference point for all your measurements in expanding the map. First though we need to determine how much we can scale up and that will depend upon the relative sizes of our paper.

We do this by measuring the distance between your central dot and a point on the boundary of the small map. Then decide how many times you can multiply that distance and still have the expanded version of the map fit on the bigger sheet. In the example opposite we are doubling our measurement.

Enlarge the grid

This next technique can help fill in those gaps fairly quickly. Any map with grid lines can be enlarged by hand; take your larger piece of paper and draw an expanded version of the grid on it. Then copy the information you need, one grid box at a time, into the larger grid as shown below.

Visit your local copy shop

Sometimes modern technology can be really helpful and worth using if the end goal justifies it. Just don't create systems that rely upon it! For instance, photocopiers are very good at taking a map at one scale and quickly enlarging it to another (though travelling to a copy shop and back may take time and energy). To use this method, identify the relevant area on your original map and have it enlarged to fill a whole page. You can then use this as the basis of a new map if the original contains a whole host of superfluous information. Simply trace over it onto another sheet of paper (the window technique works well for this too) or use the gridding process described above. Don't forget to add a scale and a north arrow if you've copied just one area from a bigger map and leave room for a key too.

This could be to just A4 and then enlarged again later, or straight to your final presentation scale and later reduced again for field mapping use.

A base map from your own measurements

If you have to create a map completely from scratch, you've a bit more work to do. Simpler technologies tend to be more reliable and/or easier to replace if they fail. Our own limbs are a given length and we can use them to make remarkably accurate measurements. Of course everyone is different, but once we're familiar with our own stride length over different terrains and gradients, we've a measure always with us that gives us 90-95% accuracy. That may not sound so good by laser standards but it's fine when designing for plants and trees. A Bunyi water level may not be an exciting technology, but its reliability comes from an unchanging law of physics – that water always finds its own level.

Sketch out a field map

To start with, sketch out a rough field map, without worrying too much about accuracy. You'll use it shortly to record distances or bearings between everything, giving you the data you'll need later to make a more accurate map. Remember that where you stand will alter your perspective, making the site look bigger side to side than front to back. Only from above can you get a true picture. So stand in the middle and make a simple pencil sketch, or if this is difficult choose the mid point of one boundary and then adjust your sketch based on a second viewpoint at approximately right angles to the first. This should give you a reasonably good starting point.

Choose your baseline

Next, plot the key fixed points on the site such as buildings, gateways, fencing corner posts, telegraph poles or big trees. Start by choosing two points, perhaps along one side and a good distance apart, from which you can measure everything else. If need be, drive in two posts yourself for this purpose. For most urban garden designs you might choose two corners of an adjacent building. Such walls are often straight, making it easy to measure between those points and so providing you with a useful baseline for your mapping.

Measure distances or take bearings

From here, the simplest method of pinpointing the other elements on the site, such as Trees 1 and 2, is to measure their distances from each corner, A and B. You can use a site tape or pacing, see the online resources for a simple pace conversion table.

This will later allow us to use trilateration to map all their positions accurately. This technique is most accurate where the directions of the measurements to any element are closest to being at right angles to each other. Therefore it's useful to choose another point that can be fairly accurately located from, that can act as a third reference point.

Mapping non-point elements

When expanding a map, any non-point element (such as a stream or pond) is more difficult to plot. The same applies when mapping a site from scratch. So far we've been measuring elements that we can pinpoint, whereas the curved bank of a pond is less easy to define. We might be able to map the point at which another element, such as a stream or a jetty interacts with it, but what about the rest of its edge? Assuming you don't have a GPS unit (this is where technology can really save you time), or an aerial photo that can give you a sense of the outline of, say a large pond or small lake, we need to consider some lower-tech methods.

We can start by pacing the circumference of a lake. We can measure the shortest distance between our already mapped points and its edge. We can take bearings from those points towards the left and right edges of the lake and to points like a jetty. We can also spend a little time sketching out its shape, from different angles. If you've someone else to work with, and your measuring tape is long enough, you could walk either side of the lake, measuring across it in different places.

These measurements combined should be enough to help you plot its shape on your map later. For large bodies of water, aerial photos can clarify the shape, though it's better to take plenty of measurements while on site in case you can't get hold of one that's sufficiently up to date.

Recording contours and any significant slope

If the site is small and essentially flat, it may not be necessary to give this much attention. However, if there are neighbouring slopes channelling water and materials towards or away from the site, these certainly need to be recorded and accounted for. Larger sites and small sloping sites will certainly need to have any gradients surveyed and contours marked.

If so:

* Use a level (e.g. A-frame, Bunyip water level, laser or dumpy level) to identify important contours and any difference in height between key elements on the site, such as the fall of streams. Remember a body of water like a lake gives you a handy level reference around its edge.

* Mark this information onto a new copy of your base map of the site through different areas of planting and terrain and mark its line upon your base map.

Take plenty of photos (or video)

These help you later with any uncertainties in your map- making, showing you valuable sight lines and saving you the need for a return visit to clarify anything you forgot to record the first time around. Of course, if your camera (or phone) has video capabilities too you can record some panoramas at the same time.

The Site Survey - making maps

Useful site surveying tools

(for mapping and gathering site information)

Simple tools (that many of us own or can make or borrow):

• Clipboard (A4 or A3)

• Clear plastic sheet/bag to keep paper dry

• Plenty of paper, or copies of the base map

• Tracing paper for information overlays

• Pens, pencils, sharpener, eraser

• Measuring tapes, rope with knots, or pacing chart

• Magnetic compass (sighting versions are best)

• Water level (small syringe useful for calibrating) or A-frame

• Soil testing charts (see online resources)

• Spades (two makes soil sampling easier)

• Jars for soil samples (tall are better, with good seals on lids)

• Bags for collecting samples

• Camera (digital is best) and spare batteries

More specialised tools:

• pH/salinity testing kits

• Sun compass

• Dumpy or outdoor rotating laser level kit

• Hand held GPS unit

• Video camera (for recording dynamic events such as strong winds or heavy rainfall)

If you're close enough to do so, take your field map home, create an accurate base map and then return to the site to record other site information. However, if you're having to create your field map and do the whole survey in just one visit, try to make your map as accurate as you can and use plenty of tracing paper for overlays. If this is the case, skip ahead now to 'Recording site information'(p56) and return here afterwards.

Decide your map scale

Useful mapmaking tools

• Drawing board

• Paper, tracing paper

• Pens (pref. technical drawing), pencils, including colours

• Eraser, sharpener

• Pair of compasses (for drawing arcs)

• Protractor, set square

• Ruler (ideally one with a selection of scales on it)

• Set of stencils

• Or for the technologically minded, Computer Aided Design combined with data points from a hand held GPS unit.

It's very easy to forget to scale down one or more measurements if you do them one at a time. In my case, forgetting to divide 10m by the scale of 50 might leave me plotting a 10cm line instead of the 20cm it should be. So it is recommended that you take your field map and do all the scale calculations first, writing them in a different coloured pen to distinguish them. Alternatively, a scale ruler allows you instead to plot everything using your original site measurements.

Draw in your chosen baseline

Next we need to create a reference from which all our other measurements can be plotted. Having calculated the scaled- down length of your baseline and the best place for it on your map, draw it in. Ideally, at this point you'd align your paper to true north first (this is convention), even though most of your measurements will be plotted from your baseline.

Plot the fixed elements

So, marking lightly at first with a pencil until you're sure your markings are correct, start adding details to your map. The methods are different, depending upon whether you took bearings or measured distances. If you took bearings, you're going to need a protractor. If instead you surveyed the site by taking measurements from either end of your baseline to each element, you'll need a pair of compasses for drawing arcs. If you don't have one, you can achieve similar results by using a long strip of paper.

Hopefully at the end of your plotting process, everything will look proportional. If so, it's time for the next stage

Plotting non-point elements

We can use a combination of these two techniques to plot the lake we were mapping earlier. Effectively we are just plotting a series of points that we'll join up to make our shape. If you had the skill to take bearings, plot these on your map first. The diagram below shows how two bearings from each point quickly define the space inside which the lake must lie.

The additional distance measurement that we took from Tree 1 helps us to define how far inside that space the north bank lies and we can do the same with the other measurements we took from our other mapped points. Having sketched an outline on site, we can now transfer that inside this space.

As an extra, you can scale down the circumference that you measured, cut a piece of thread to that length, join its ends together and lay it out on your map until the shape looks right before tracing the outline onto the paper

What if I forgot to measure something?

Don't worry; making mistakes is the quickest way to learn. This is where your photos help.

Climate and landform

That said, if the eco-system you're designing in is an unfamiliar one, you'll first need to gain an understanding of the local geology and climate. What you may take for granted at home may be completely absent there. We'd be wise to never make any assumptions about what will and won't work in any given place, even in familiar landscapes. Ultimately, the strategies we choose to apply will have to be suited to the local resources and limitations. For instance, in really cold climates, frost might often fill whole valleys and be a more important limiting factor than wind in the planting of orchards, leading to them being located high up on slopes in those places.

Scale of the project

Another factor that will determine your approach is the size of the site. A small garden design will elicit a completely different approach from that for a broadacre farm. While for most of us the former is the most likely place we'll find ourselves working, there's no shortage of farms in desperate need of a redesign. Thankfully, the likes of Darren Doherty and Joel Salatin are showing us better ways under the banner of Regenerative Agriculture and we may all soon find ourselves offering our design services to farms as well. Bill Mollison suggests that the first thing you should do when arriving on site is to get to the highest point and consider the landscape from there. I think it safe to say that if you only have a small garden that he doesn't mean to get up on your roof, but on a broadacre plot this strategy can give you a clear overview of the terrain.

Now, if you've ever tried to dig a pond by hand you'll know how much energy it takes to change the landscape. That's why it's useful when designing broadacre properties to consider Yeoman's Keyline Scale of Permanence.

This scale reminds us of the relative permanence of the main systems we'll be interacting with; the most permanent (un- changable) being at the top of the list. Bill Mollison and David Holmgren suggest an adaptation to P. A. Yeoman's original scale when planning permacultural systems:

1. Climate 2. Landform 3. Water supply 4. Roads 5. Plant systems 6. Microclimates 7. Buildings

8. Subdivisional fences (fields) 9. Soil

Given that climate takes a lot to change (though we're having a good go at it) and the landscape can only be easily modified to a small degree, this means designing water systems first, which define the placement of roads, then trees and so on. Given that water moves across a site away from the highest point and at right angles to contour it's an important location to start from.

Collecting data

Now using your field map or more accurate base map, start collecting data. Rather than cluttering up your map with all of this, you can use overlays† to record the different types of information. Place one onto your base map and trace out the boundary corners and north arrow. Doing this will enable you to reposition it onto the base map accurately later. If you instead use copies of the base map, then start with one of those. Give each a title that identifies the type of information you're recording on it. Even if you use base map copies during your survey, you can still create overlays later from the collected data. Note: your original field versions may be quite rough and not as pretty as those examples shown on the following pages. Some of the following site observations can be mapped. Additional information can be recorded on a separate sheet.¤

Record existing site elements

* What's the primary land use on the site?

* By way of a comparison, what is the primary agriculture /traditional crop in this area?

This information may help you to identify what already grows well here. However, don't allow that to make you any less observant about the specific conditions on this particular site.

Examine all boundaries (walls, hedges, fences, waterways etc.). Note what they are made of and how well they are being maintained. Make a note to find out who owns each one.

Now add to copies of your map or overlays all the main elements currently found on or making use of the site. Use the PASTE acronym to help you remember everything:

* What Plants and trees are growing on the site: on the land and in any bodies of water? You might record a transect† across the site as part of this process. Note any fungi you find too – while they're more closely related to the animal kingdom, there is no F in this acronym.

* What Animals (domesticated and wild mammals, birds, insects, fish etc.) are using the site? Look for any signs of their activities. Don't forget about

humans either.

* What Structures are there (e.g. buildings, greenhouse, shed, paving, pond, dam, terracing, wind turbine pole etc.)?

What condition are they in? Are they all being used to their full potential? Any archaeological or sacred sites?

* What Tools are being used here (e.g. wind turbine, pole lathe, washing line etc.)? What work is done here?

* What Events take place here (e.g. social: parties, courses, camps – or natural: floods, frost, fire etc.)?

You may not be able to identify every tree, plant, fungus or animal track. This is another time when photos can be useful. Otherwise, if there's enough to spare, collect a leaf or flower for identification later, either by the client, another gardener, or by referring to a book.

Rain gulley, animal track or both?

A path along which one records and counts occurrences of the phenomena of study (e.g. plants, noting each instance).

With any plant or tree species, you could also record them using the DAFOR framework, noting the relative abundance of species in a particular area. The letters stand for Dominant, Abundant, Frequent, Occasional and Rare. Using this you can quickly describe the overall flora of a site without having to count any individual species. Some experienced botanists also add a 'Missing' category, for those species they are surprised not to find. Remember though that what you see above ground changes through the seasons, and that you may only be able to survey the site at one point in the cycle.

Map access points and routes through the site

Using either an overlay or a new copy of the base map, record the access points for people, animals and any vehicles too. Are they adequate for potential site developments and also in good repair? In particular check the state of any bridges or similar structures. Check access roads to the site and the areas they travel through. In fire risk areas, you'll want a safe escape route, not one passing through a potential inferno.

Identify the different zones on the site

Zoning is all about how energy is being used on the site. We'll start by mapping current patterns of activity and later redesign for greater efficiency. Zones are focused upon main areas of use such as buildings (often called zone 0) and any well-used desire lines, where people move slowly enough to notice what's going on around them. To minimise work we'll later gather the things needing the most attention around these focuses.

Now sketch out the current zoning onto your desire lines and access map or overlay. Using a different colour for each zone is a great way of differentiating them, like in my example below.

The desire lines around my mobile home shaped my zoning of the space 60

The Site Survey - recording information

Conventionally, to define the different zones on a broadacre site we'd follow this rough guide:

Zone 1 – Closest to the home, especially any access points (front and back doors), also alongside regularly used paths. Where most intensive gardening and social use occurs.

Zone 2 – Gets a bit less attention; may be further away, but still perhaps intensively gardened. May include soft fruit, fruit trees, small animals, etc.

Zone 3 – Commercial production (less intensive) e.g grains, main crop vegetables, orchards, agroforestry, fodder crops, pasture, meadow etc.

Zone 4 – Managed woodland (often to stabilise steep slopes): timber, coppice, fuel, forage etc.

Zone 5 – Places we humans rarely visit (only to observe and to learn). Where wildlife moves freely.

We'll not necessarily identify all five external zones in this space, especially if the site is relatively small (e.g. an average garden). We'll almost certainly find areas that we can designate as zone 1 and possibly 2, along with zone 5 areas for wildlife; even if these are limited only to drains, gutters and a patch of wild plants. We shouldn't forget that roofs, the tops of trees and inside hedges also act as good zone 5 areas.

With larger sites, especially broadacre farms, we'll also be able to identify zones 3 and 4. Depending upon the site, you may notice that zone 0 (the central focus of activity) isn't a constant, but moves seasonally. This could be the case in a community garden, where the social hub may be a passively warmed greenhouse in the winter, but switch to a shadier spot during the summer. You may also identify more than one zone 0 in regular use on a site, such as a home and a workshop.†

In urban areas, regularly used community spaces such as schools and colleges, allotments, libraries and leisure centres may be considered in zones 2, 3 or 4 depending on their proximity. Remember, at this stage we're just identifying the zones as we observe the space currently being used. You may well identify opportunities to say, turn a zone 2 into a zone 1, but your job for now is to just record the site's use as it currently stands.

While zones are all about conserving energy on site, sectors are all about the energy coming in from the outside. Often called wild energies (as they tend to be beyond our control to do much about outside the site boundaries), these provide us with many opportunities to obtain a yield. Ultimately, all energy flows from a source to a sink and sometimes our site is in between. The energy source is almost always the sun, even though it may have arrived on site in the form of wind or water flow. Our aim is to harvest, store and cycle energy as much as possible before it's lost again from our system.

Map the different sectors of the site

Follow the same technique as before to map out the sectors on the site. Given enough overlay/tracing paper, I would use at least two sheets, maybe more. The reason for this is that later on when we do our analysis, we may be considering different combinations of these influences during the placement of each element. We may need to consider the influences of wind and flooding for one element, whereas for another our concerns may be sun and water availability. So ideally use a sheet for each sector, but I'd suggest that if you are to combine sectors onto overlays to save paper, to group them like this:

* Those sectors that are directional, their angle varying little across the site (e.g. sun, wind etc.).

* Those sectors that are topographical: mapped onto specific areas of the site (e.g. frost, flooding etc.).

Inclement weather

Whenever it's wet or cold or windy, we usually get indoors as soon as we can. However, it's just that kind of uncomfortable weather that can give us the most important information about a site. One permaculture approach is to design for disasters, and it's important for us to become aware of seasonal weather extremes and their patterns so we can plan for them. Unusual weather events can provide us with insights into these potential issues as they reveal a whole collection of things that we don't normally see, such as:

Heavy rain – Where is water being focussed? How does it flow down slopes? Are there signs of erosion where water is flowing quickly? How does rain flow off roofs? Are there any leaking or missing gutters? Does water infiltrate any buildings? Are there any overflowing drains? Where does water puddle (this can also be a clue to soil compaction)? Are watercourses coloured brown by soil being washed off fields? By the time you've learned the answers to these questions you're likely to be quite wet, but you'll have learned a lot about your site.

Water run off erosion gulley

Strong winds – Where are the windiest areas? Are there any places where litter is blown in circles? Or never settles on the ground? Where are the most sheltered spots? Poles with simple flags (e.g. carrier bags) placed around a site can enable you to observe wind patterns across a large area from a distance.

Drought – When rain is scarce, which areas are most affected by the lack of water? Where is heat and drying out most prevalent? What happens during the first fall of rain after a dry spell – does soil capping prevent the efficient infiltration of water into the soil? Is this problem worse on steeper gradients?

Where is moisture retained the longest in the soil (fungi are a big clue to this)?

Frost – Where does frost settle? Is cold air trapped and unable to move down-slope, by hedges, walls or buildings? Could this be remedied? Are there frost-free areas around trees, under hedges, or around buildings? Go out early in the morning to view this – a few hours later the remaining frost may no longer remain in the really cold places, only where shade prevents the morning sun from melting it.

Frost pocket: The downhill flow of cold air off the moorland plateau is interrupted by the building, which is in turn chilled by the trapped air

Snow – The thaw after snow shows us more than we can normally see. Snow melts more quickly on the roofs of heated buildings that are poorly insulated. Capped wells and other underground bodies of water will melt snow more quickly than surrounding ground; a clear circle on a snowy yard is probably an old well that has been concreted over. Other favourable microclimates, such as around buildings, will also thaw snow quickly. Conversely, the chilliest spots will hang onto snow residues the longest. Desire lines are also easy to see in the snow. Where do people and animals prefer to walk? Now you know!

Fire – Hopefully you'll never experience a wildfire, by all accounts it's a pretty terrifying thing. If the site is in a fire risk area then designing to protect the site against it is a priority (remember designing for disasters?). Instead of waiting for one, find out about the history of wildfires in the area and their patterns. Radiant heat is the most destructive aspect of fire and burns from a considerable distance, even a small campfire can force a retreat. The main things to look for on site are:

* Inflammable plants and trees; conifers and eucalypts (high resin content trees) burn particularly fiercely. Do prevailing winds blow on to the site from that direction?

* Is the site on a slope? Fire travels very quickly uphill and is fiercest on ridges, which are usually the driest areas.

* Where are access roads to the site routed?

* Is there an emergency on-site gravity-fed water supply?

* What are the buildings made of? Are they designed with fire-protection in mind (e.g. white painted, with door and window screens, simple roof shapes and screened undershot guttering that doesn't collect hot ashes, etc.)?

Solar elevation angle

Doing this will help you find different microclimates on site, together with opportunities to harvest incoming energies and areas of the site that need protection from them. Remember that some sectors have vertical components too and can vary

in strength with altitude. Low winter sun can be blocked by tall trees and buildings, so it's useful to be able to approxi- mate and record their heights, to estimate seasonal shade patterns. The Sun compass also allows you to estimate this changing shade using the angles printed on the back (see below).

Estimating heights

You may be concerned about the shade a building or tree will throw in the winter, or want to know the protected distance offered by a windbreak, so it's useful to be able to estimate the heights of tall objects. The simplest method involves comparing the height of say a tree, with a person standing beneath it. This can be pretty accurate where the tree is only a few times the height of the person. An adaptation of this is to compare the length of your own shadow with the tall object. Pacing works pretty well for this, though if the ground is uneven or of changing slope, this can distort the result.

Record water across the site

* Are there any open bodies of water present on the site (ponds, lakes, reservoirs etc.)? Any opportunities in the landscape for creating more (especially in clay soils)?

* Any water passing through the site (streams, rivers etc.)?

* Are there any drainage ditches or earthworks?

* Any signs of wells/boreholes or monitoring of aquifer levels?

* Estimate the surface area of any roofs and note which of them have guttering and to where they drain rainwater.

* How much water storage is there currently on site for different uses (drinking, washing, flushing, irrigation etc.)?

* How much is stored in tanks, butts etc.? How long do these last during drought? – a question for the client.

* How are water systems connected on site? What water cycling is currently taking place?

* Is grey or black water being treated before leaving the site?

Take at least one soil sample

What do the locally abundant wild plants tell you about the soil? Before digging a hole, use the indicator plants chart¤ to determine what kind of soil these plants like to grow in.

Choose sites to survey away from compacted areas like paths and roads.

To see how accurate this is, get a copy of the Biological and Soil Monitoring Chart¤ and a spade or two. Then:

* Find a suitable site, away from compacted areas like access points or pathways.

* Start filling in the chart, starting with column 1 for site 1.

* Sketch a cross section and mark the location on it.

* First make a note of the current land use there.

* Determine the degree of plant diversity – to do this properly you might use a one metre square frame (or a hula hoop!) and study just what is inside. Record or sample plants.

* Record any signs of insect, spider and soil life activity (worm casts, nibbled leaves, webs etc).

* Now dig your soil profile (a square hole a spade's width on each side and a spade blade deep). How easy is it to dig? – This is a clue to the degree of compaction!

* Carefully remove an additional downward 'slice' to one side. Sandwiching it with a second spade can help to lift it out. Observe the different soil layers, roots and soil life.

* Smear a little soil onto the chart (in the colour box).

* Taking a representative sample of topsoil use the 'How to test soil texture' flowchart¤ and follow the instructions until you have determined your soil type.

* To check this, also perform the jar test¤ on a further sample from the same place. This picture clearly shows the layer of settled sand that falls straight to the bottom, with silt quickly settling out over the next 30 minutes or so on top of it. The paler clay is still in suspension on the top and may be for many days or even weeks in the case of really fine clays.

If your site has a variety of different microclimates and land uses, it's worth surveying the soil in a few places and then comparing your findings. What do these observations tell you about the underlying geology of this area? The base rock will determine the soil type and thus the basic growing conditions.†

Identify the site's remaining limiting factors

Our survey may have already identified some of the site's key limiting factors: perhaps excessively shady or boggy areas, very heavy or light soil, or crops regularly grazed off by insects or wild animals? Some of these factors we may seek to modify, others such as altitude we are going to have to accept and seek to discover the gifts they offer. Our role as designer is to identify key limiting factors, and then to design strategies to overcome them. Sometimes, by removing one limitation, the landscape will change dramatically, like removing grazing animals from a landscape to permit the regrowth of forest. Returning to our leaky barrel analogy, an effective strategy might be as simple as plugging some of those wasteful leaks. A quick look around many sites will quickly identify the tragic loss of energy and resources such as:

Chris Dixon in his woodland, which regenerated after sheep were removed

* Heat escaping from buildings.

* Fertility being washed out of the soil.

* Water leaving the site before being fully utilised.

* Crops being left to rot (most commonly under trees).

* High maintenance, low output systems (e.g. most lawns).

* Vandalism.

You may also identify other opportunities being wasted like:

* Workers having insufficient to do, or being wasted on low value tasks. Volunteer help not being made use of.

* Free or cheap local resources, not being collected or utilised.

In addition there may be other 'non-physical' limiting factors to consider, such as:

* Legislation (e.g. planning, conservation etc.).

* Ownership.

* Cultural issues (including the reactions of neighbours).

Explore them as part of your client interview process. A mind map of limiting factors in the online resources will help you identify others that relate to your site.

Map any site utilities

Are any mains services (gas, electricity, sewage, water, phone etc.) already being supplied to the site? Where are they, above or below ground? If the latter isn't clear, then utility company maps can help identify the routes of buried pipes and cables. This will help you to avoid accidentally damaging any during excavations. In which parts of the site are such utilities available or easily connected up to?

Where is the nearest settlement?

Where can resources be obtained for site development (e.g. building materials)? Where are the nearest shops for food? Where can medical help be obtained in an emergency?

Identify any free or cheap resources available

Finally we need to record the valuable resources available on or close to the site. These may include natural resources such as timber that can be harvested sustainably. Space is a resource that many people don't have, so any buildings standing unused offer the opportunity for new ventures, including renting them out to other businesses or as a venue for running courses.

These non-physical limitations can be considered sectors too, as legislation can change unexpectedly making current site systems untenable. One example being a successful juicing business, built up over many years, by buying fruit from abandoned, unsprayed orchards. Then one day their main customer decided that everything they sold must be certified organic. This seemingly good decision meant the farm had to find a new source of fruit and abandon those old orchards to a possible grubbing out.

There may be specialist machinery available nearby that could be leased, and local people with specific expertise that can be employed to help develop aspects of the site.

Often items considered to be junk by most people can be put to ingenious use. Remember, the problem is the solution – it's only the way we look at things that makes them a problem or an asset. Here are a few examples:

* Tyres being made into rodent-proof wormeries (of course, if you have enough, you could even build your own Earthship dwelling!).

* Old baths being turned into small ponds and all kinds of other large containers used to store rainwater.

* Pallets made into compost bins.

* Patio doors, recycled plumbing bits and old copper pipe being made into very efficient solar hot water panels.

* Double glazing units thrown out by window companies made into greenhouses/bioshelters.

* Large plastic bottles (from cooking oil, water etc.) being made into cloches.

When travelling to and from the site, make a note of any local businesses that may be throwing away useful items, such as any of the above and also:

* Cardboard (for mulching).

* Green waste (for making compost).

* Manure (need I explain this one?).

* Glass bottles (make good raised bed-edging).

* Waste timber (for building garden structures).

And so on... We are limited only by our imagination! So make a note of everything that's available on the site, or that you've noticed nearby. Any of it may become an integral part of your design.

Once you're back at home again, you can turn your rough field data into bigger and clearer overlays. As previously mentioned, if you have plenty of tracing paper it will give you the most flexibility in making decisions later. Remember. if you need to group different data onto single overlays, then try to keep directional and topographical sectors on separate sheets.

Place each fresh overlay sheet in turn over the base map and unless it's to record only directional information, first mark on several points to locate it (corners of boundaries or buildings are ideal). Then transfer across, a sheet at a time, all of the information you've gathered from your rough field maps or overlays. I find when doing this that a good dark pen is useful for defining boundaries and that using plenty of colour shading helps to show up different areas, such as zones.

Remember that directional sectors such as the sun's path, don't need to be the full size of the map. You may wish to centre them on different points of interest when you're later making decisions, so a little smaller can be more convenient

Choosing systems and elements

Ideally, we'll only be including systems and elements in our design if they fulfil at least three functions. Remember the ecological principle: Multiple functions for each element. Nature happens to be so productive, because everything does so many things (take a moment to think of all the services trees provide). So we might design a road to also be a firebreak and a means of harvesting and directing rainwater into a dam. This saves both space on the ground and the additional cost of extra earthworks. It's also important to ensure that there's a diversity of elements in your design, providing security – especially for important functions like food, water, energy etc. Remember: Multiple elements for each important function. If all our energy is supplied from one source (e.g. mains electricity) and that provision fails, then we're in trouble. If we don't have multiple sources to meet all our important needs, then we're very vulnerable.

Financial costs

Locally sourced materials were once the easiest and cheapest to use, which is why older buildings tend to blend into their environment so well. Sadly the use of cheap overseas labour and fossil fuel-driven mass production means that's not always the case now. Earth-friendly choices are often more financially expensive, locally grown organic food being a good example. We do however also have the restraint of a financial budget to consider and our task is to create a design within it.

Given that nothing is certain, I'd consider alternative options in the possible event of the client's available funds being either significantly increased or reduced at some point in the future. If you can offer 'plan B's to the client, it would add flexibility to your design. Also, while budgeting, consider how costs can be reduced by timely intervention (plugging leaks – 'a stitch in time saves nine') or by buying cheaper options (e.g. seeds as opposed to plants). Indeed your whole implementation plan could be affected by strategies used to reduce costs.

Being able to cost a project is a really valuable skill, especially if you have any intention of designing professionally for other people. Don't forget though that for some clients time is their greatest limiting factor.

Time limitations

You should rule out any systems that will take too long to put in place, though a renegotiation of the project deadline might be worthwhile if an idea is a particularly good one.

Ultimately, being able to estimate how much time and money each phase of a design may require, will stand you in good stead. Getting into the habit of recording both the financial and time costs of any project you do, will make it easier for you to give estimates to future clients. If for instance, you know the time and materials used in making a raised bed of a given size, you can multiply those figures to obtain a reasonably accurate 'guesstimate' for other similar situations. As with all these things, practice makes perfect.

Appropriate scale

Consider what systems and elements would be best suited to the size of any site. A treebog would probably be too big for most urban gardens, while forest garden techniques could still be applied there using fan, cordon or espaliered trees. Ponder too the required capacity of systems.

Interconnectedness

By identifying the needs (inputs) and yields (products/outputs) of each system or element, we can identify where beneficial relationships can be created. If we can connect two elements together so that the outputs of one feed the needs of another, we are well on the way to creating a self-sustaining system. The more we can do this, the less work will be required to maintain the overall system we design.

Needs and yields (input/output) analysis

The classic textbook example is the 'Permaculture chicken', where its needs, products and (intrinsic) behaviours are all considered. The ideal is to meet all its needs on site, make use of its behaviours to reduce work and also to make use of its additional outputs (e.g. manure), so avoiding pollution.

In order to identify possible beneficial connections, we need to do this for each key element in the system. As a result, this is a process that can take some time, but the time and energy that can be saved by good design is far greater. Our ultimate aim with this is to connect each of our best choice elements into a mutually supporting cycle. We'll return to this in the section on placement and integration, but for now we can use it to help us choose the most appropriate elements (e.g. plants, animals, structures, tools etc.) for our system.

Two other useful tools to help you identify elements most likely to integrate well with other parts of your design are 'random assembly' and the 'web of connections'. What we learn from these can also be of use to us when deciding about placements in the next section.

Placement

Now we'll experiment with best placements for the different elements and systems in our design. If there's a fixed point of focus on the site (such as a house), then we'll be placing everything most efficiently in relation to that. However, when starting with a 'blank canvas' we get to choose the best place to site our centre of activity. If we're arranging our design around a proposed new house or other structure, its placement will probably be our most important decision. If we're designing a site without an obvious central element, then we'll need to identify the most important elements to place first and go from there.

Around an existing main element

When designing around a fixed point of focus like a building, we've a number of methods we can use to plan the layout of the site. Using our base map and overlays from the survey, we'll aim to make our mistakes 'on paper', instead of in the landscape itself. One helpful tool for this process is the land- scape modelling technique.

Laying out an approximate model of the site on a floor or table using cushions, cloth and ropes, gives us a 3D space into which we can explore placement of our systems and elements. We can use the same cards we made earlier for 'random assembly', to represent elements, and by moving them about, explore the relationships between them. Creating a model can give us a landscape overview that we don't get from ground level. Imagine you're 5,000 feet tall or flying over the landscape in a hot-air balloon. Now, consider the following factors in turn to identify the best location for each system or element.

Design from patterns to details

Before looking at the finer details of your design, establish an overall pattern. This will be guided by many of the factors that follow. It's important to adapt your design to the opportunities the site offers, rather than trying to adapt the site to the design (a common human strategy now we use fossil fuels to replace skill with brute force!). You may be excited about creating a forest garden, or growing olives, but on an inappropriate site you'll be wasting time and energy fighting nature. For instance, hilly and mountainous regions are excellent for storing water high in the landscape, where it can then be made to do work (e.g. hydro-electric power generation or irrigation), but not so good for growing tender crops. Identify the opportunities the site offers and design to take best advantage of them.

Microclimates

This may seem like jumping straight ahead to the small stuff, but microclimates actually come in all shapes and sizes. The whole of Britain is a microclimate, benefiting as it does from the warm ocean currents delivered by the North Atlantic drift. South-westerly prevailing winds bring plenty of rain and the west of Britain receives more of it than the east. In turn, Dartmoor, the area of high moorland in the south-west region, has even more rainfall than its surroundings. Focusing in further, we can pick any of the valleys on the moor and find sunnier and shadier aspects, windier and sheltered spots, damper and drier areas. Look closer and you'll continue to see variations, until you pick up a single stone and find creatures there that like the dark and damp conditions it provides. Our job as designers is to spot these opportunities and place things there that will make the best use of the gifts they offer.

Elevation planning and aspect

By considering the altitude of a site and any slopes present, we can identify the diverse microclimates, opportunities and limiting factors that occur there. There are specific strategies that work best at each point on a slope, such as using trees to stabilise steep gradients and having vulnerable food crops growing above the frost line. The thermal belt between frosty hilltops and valley bottoms in cool temperate zones offers a slightly longer growing season. The aspect of a slope is also a factor to consider. For instance, growing conditions near the top of a sun-facing slope can equate roughly to those at the bottom on the shady side of the same hill. In other words, the extra sun compensates for the limitations of the higher altitude (temperature drops about 0.5°C for every 100 metres above sea level).

So how do the design elements need to be arranged in relation to slope? If we want anything to flow under gravity through a system, we'll need of course to place them at the correct relative heights. To move water from roof guttering, into a raised tank, then a toilet cistern, on to a septic tank and finally a wetland

Zoning

Systems and elements that need the most attention are of course best placed close to our central focus, where we spend most of our time. Start by identifying which elements in your design will need most attention. Do this by thinking about how often a particular thing needs to be visited, either to clean, repair or harvest from it. A chicken shed for instance should need at least two visits a day: to let out and shut in the chickens. In addition there may be separate daily visits to collect eggs. Cleaning occurs perhaps a couple of times a week. Shed maintenance may be a few times a year. By way of contrast, a compost heap might have fresh green waste deliveries from the kitchen only every few days, need turning about once every ten days (for hot systems) and be visited a few times in the spring to harvest the compost. From this we begin to notice that some tasks take place on a daily basis and others may be more seasonal. Use this information to place elements needing most attention closest to your central point. This is a good general rule to follow, though there are exceptions, as we'll discover in the next section.

Access and desire lines

Access points and desire lines will influence the basic circular zoning pattern; regularly walked routes can also be considered as zone 1, allowing any higher maintenance systems to be sited there. Driveways are given less attention as a driver's mind is often on where they're going, or what they'll need to do on arrival at home, so design them as low maintenance areas. Conversely, you might deliberately place high maintenance systems or points of interest where they create new advantageous desire lines. An attractive new feature in a previously neglected area will get more attention, making extra zone 1 space along the path leading there.

Don't make that path too straight though if you want people to slow down and interact with elements along the way. We obtain further benefits by creating new desire lines for other creatures too. Place a high pole in the middle of an open area where you're growing vegetables to encourage birds of prey. By giving them somewhere to perch, they can help to manage rodent populations for you as another part of your Integrated Pest Management strategy. Sometimes the best placement of elements can make life so much easier. Consider how much less work it is to herd animals if gates are placed in the corners of fields instead of half way along a side.

Sectors

Now let's consider how incoming wild energies, such as wind, water and sunlight, might interact with each of our chosen systems and elements, which we can position to either harvest those energies most effectively, or to shelter other elements from them. Often, the best placements for creating a yield are where wild energies are already being focused, such as harvest- ing water by building a dam where an area of sloping land directs run off towards a Keypoint (arrowed). Notice how much larger the trees are, both there and in the valley below, as the water and the fertility it carries starts to settle out on the gentler slopes. As it takes a lot of energy to change the landscape (remember the Scale of Permanence), it's far easier to work with the existing terrain

In a similar way, upslope wind is compressed and accelerated towards the brow of hills by the rising ground below. We can use this to our advantage by placing wind turbines there. This is an example of harvesting the energy of a sector. Of course, when considering most buildings, we'd instead be looking to provide shelter from those winds to reduce heat loss. In the higher latitudes, it's also important not to block low winter sunlight from coming into buildings, so aim to keep that sector clear of anything that would reduce it. Compromises often have to be made though, such as between allowing all winter sunlight to reach a building and completely protecting it from prevailing winds. In Britain the latter come from the south-west, which is also the direction of the midwinter sunset. Which you choose to favour will probably depend on additional factors. Certainly for plants and trees, wind is the main limiting factor to growth and for pollination by insects, which don't fly when it's windy. Thus it can be a good trade off to sacrifice a little sunlight for a good windbreak.

A similar issue arises where a good connection exists between two elements that need to be physically close together, but prefer different microclimates.

Low voltage wind turbines are often used to provide power to buildings, though the windy conditions that suit energy generation can reduce the energy efficiency of any building. Placing them further apart in order to overcome this increases the distance the electricity has to be transmitted, which for low voltages can result in high losses. This leads us instead to considering larger, higher voltage wind turbines more suited to serving a collection of dwellings.

To give an example here of the importance of good placement: some orchards use energy-hungry giant fans to stop cold air settling on blossoms and ruining the crop. Nature wouldn't put those trees in that frosty microclimate and if we want to avoid a whole heap of wasted energy, neither should we. Lastly, consider how to protect and enhance any highly valued sectors on the site like good views and places of tranquillity and how those unwanted sectors like bad views, noise and pollution can be moderated by good placements. Sometimes a system or element's ideal spot can be determined by simply noticing its optimum zone, sector and elevation.

Soil type

That said, when considering plants and trees, growing them in the right soil type is also important, so this is where we review what we learned from our observations. If soil conditions vary across the site, then we've a greater diversity of opportunities for growing. As gardeners we're often told that an ideal soil is a good fertile loam with a pH around 6.5, but if the soil was like that everywhere we'd see far fewer species around us. The Earth's varying soil conditions lead to a diversity of ecosystems containing a multitude of species and that extra diversity leads to more beneficial relationships, making the whole web of life stronger. Diversity creates stability.

Now, the evaluation of zones and sectors may suggest growing a particular plant in a given place, but if the soil is of insufficient fertility, the wrong pH, or too wet or dry, we should probably think again. It's always easier to find plants best suited to the local soil (as nature does), than to try and modify it. That said, sometimes (with extremely acid soils in particular) it may be worth the investment of time and resources† to modify pH, at least in a small area, as part of a general soil improvement strategy for intensive food growing. This is almost always the case for zone 1.

Utilities

Don't forget that any elements needing mains utilities (e.g. electricity, gas, water, sewage, telephone etc.) will need placing where they can be easily connected, unless of course the benefit of choosing a particular site outweighs the cost of extending cables or pipes.

Visualise succession

Nature never stands still. Trees grow and throw more shade, microclimates emerge and habitats change. Old trees fall down, rivers change course and then there's climate change to consider. Depending upon the timescale of our design, these may be things that we need to consider when deciding placements. Particularly if those resources are unused by-products such as wood ash.

Observing the landscape and visualising succession enables us to anticipate changing conditions and create a design that evolves to take advantage of them. This is a skill increasingly acquired with experience. Sometimes the client's vision includes distinct phases. For example, an initial focus may be on erecting a dwelling, but with need for an intensive food-producing garden at the same time. You might start by placing the garden safely out of the way of building work, and only move it to zone 1 once the building is complete. A forest garden could then be established where the intensive garden previously was, suggesting the planting of young fruit trees there from the beginning and establishing the intensive food garden around them. Visualising the development of a site gives us clues that can help us accelerate the succession of any systems we install.

Incremental design

"Allow the system to demonstrate its own evolution." - Bill Mollison

A design drawing only provides a snapshot of how a site might look at a specific stage in its evolution, so visualise how the site is likely to mature. In addition, the needs of the client may also change. They may develop an increased dependency upon the site for food or resources, either due to scarcity of them in shops or a greater number of mouths to feed.

Future proofing: a new orchard at Ragman's Lane Farm, planted to reduce their reliance on buying in apples for their successful juicing business

Perhaps surpluses from other local growers reduce their income from what were previously high-value crops, forcing a change of direction? New people may bring new ideas. The site may be required to fulfil extra or different functions. Neighbours may change and this may bring an increased risk of pollution from the surrounding environment. Some changes can be anticipated and some cannot. By involving the client(s) as much as possible during the design process, we ensure that they're better able to observe the evolution of the design over time and to respond accordingly. A design can never be completely finished, as it will get tweaked over time to improve its performance.

An example of this is the Welsh 3,000s race, a route of around 26 miles from the top of Snowdon to Foel Fras, including some 13,000ft of ascent and 14 summits over 3,000ft. Over the years, people have tried varying the route in different ways to shave a little time off the record. Each new successful variation improves the design, but as there are an infinite number of fine tunings that can be made, the perfect route may never be found. This is classic incremental design.

The fine details...

Once we've laid out the basic pattern for the whole site, we can start to look at the finer details of each system; this is where we create our planting plans and so on. It's useful now to take our ideas and start trying them out on the site to check they work in more than just theory. By laying out our plan on the ground, using ropes, hoses or stakes as markers, we can get a sense of how our proposal looks in the real world. Invite your clients to walk around the pathways, ideally for a week or so, and then give you feedback (this could be done by moving the markers). Confirm it all when it feels right to everyone.

Implementation

So we are almost at the point now where we can impose our design ideas upon the real world, but first we need to create an implementation plan to guide us.

Breaking down the task

We'll start by breaking down the whole process into its major sub-tasks, creating more manageable chunks. These may already be very clear from our design process. For a simple design, or where you are both designer and client, this may be adequate enough for you to work from. For more complex designs, you may already have created a design around specific phases, each one with its own budget, deadline or SMART goal, and map. Whatever degree of complexity we start with, we'll want to divide up each sub-task to create a Work Breakdown Structure (WBS).

Start small and work out from well-managed areas

Set realistic goals – many small successes make you and the client feel good and create added enthusiasm for the project. As you can see, the WBS forms a branching pattern, starting with the end objective at the top.

Sub-tasks are then connected to this and in turn divided up into smaller tasks, components and so on, until each part is a man- ageable size. This forms the basis of our plan, though a WBS doesn't identify priorities or the timing of activities.

Factors that influence task prioritisation

In order to start prioritising tasks, we need to consider all the factors that might influence this. The following can help you decide what should be done when, and identify where certain tasks depend upon the completion of others. I usually consider them in this order:

Least change for greatest effect

What little thing can you do that will create the most benefit from the time or resources invested? Of course, what constitutes 'little' will vary depending upon the scale of the project. Often this might be plugging a leak, such as a regular loss of soil, money, or energy. Building soils for instance can reduce the need for irrigation, which can save money on earthworks or other irrigation infrastructure. It's always easier to conserve energy than use up resources to generate more. Small investments that save you money or resources in the longer term (e.g. building insulation) can free up additional funds to make bigger money- saving investments in the future. Early successes can encourage further action, so give your client an instant payback and let them see the value of your design advice.

Design around the limiting factors

Seasonal constraints must be considered when planting trees or sowing crops. If trees are required and money is also a limiting factor, bare-rooted trees become a good investment. They are cheaper to buy than pot grown trees, but can only be planted safely during the colder winter months, so two limiting factors combine to give high priority to winter tree planting. Likewise, if you want a good harvest from your garden in the autumn, there's a fairly small window of time (in the spring) in which to sow most of your crops. Seeds are cheaper than plants. Remember McHarg's exclusion method ? We can also apply the concept to time. Identify your most important or most difficult or time-constrained tasks and then put them onto your calendar first.

Resource availability

Many limiting factors can become surpluses at other times. For many people with a land-based income, money is much more abundant in the summer and autumn than in the winter. Conversely though, time may become a key resource when there's a lot less to do in the garden. Jobs that require a lot of finance or labour should be done when these surpluses are available. A surplus of labour may also bring extra skills. If the site is suitable, running courses is a good way to take advantage of this. As well as potentially providing a financial yield, a practical course can also bring in an expert and a lot of keen volunteer labour to get a big project done.

Dependencies (a.k.a. precedences)

There are certain things that need to be completed, or at least part-completed, before others can be started. A building needs its foundations laid before its roof is put on, or to make a sandwich you first need to bake the bread. These are called causal dependencies. However there are other factors that can determine the pace at which a project can proceed. Sometimes the availability of resources is the key limiting factor and sometimes it simply makes sense from an organisational perspective to arrange tasks in a certain order. For example, you may have a particularly skilled person on site, who can do two distinct tasks not normally implemented at the same time. These are discretionary dependencies. The key thing of course is to remember to place any dependent activities on the timeline after those that they are dependent upon